Chelsey Halal
Presented to:

Mom
Presented by:

January 27, 2010
Date:

Every *child* born into the world

is a new thought of God,

an *ever-fresh* and

radiant possibility.

Kate Douglas Wiggin

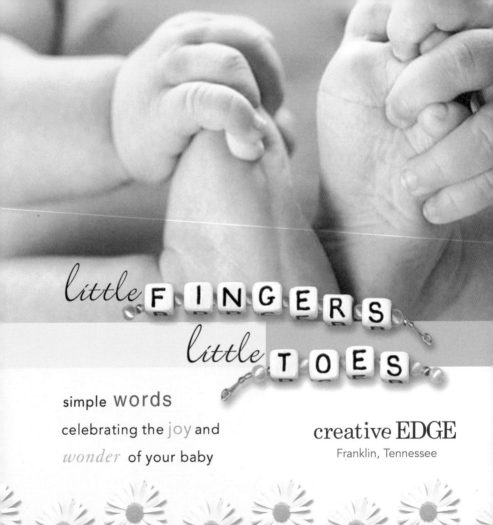

little **FINGERS**
little **TOES**

simple **words**
celebrating the joy and
wonder of your baby

creative **EDGE**
Franklin, Tennessee

Babies are **beautiful**, wonderful,

exciting, enchanting,

extraordinary little creatures—who

grow up into ordinary folk like us.

Doris Dyson

I can't think why *mothers love* them.

All *babies* do is leak at both ends.

Douglas Feaver

Let Your mercy, O LORD, be upon us,
Just as we hope in You.

Psalm 33:22 NKJV

Long to grow up into the fullness of your salvation; cry for this as a baby cries for his milk.

1 Peter 2:2 TLB

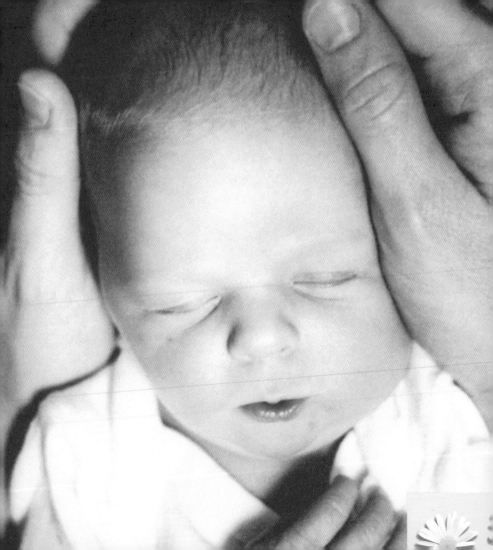

A baby: the *tiniest* thing

I ever decided

to put my *whole life* into.

I live my life in this earthly body
by trusting in the Son of God,
who loved me and gave
himself for me.

Galatians 2:20 NLT

Like a warrior's fistful of arrows are the children of a vigorous youth. Oh, how blessed are you parents, with your quivers full of children!

Psalm 127:4–5 THE MESSAGE

little TOES

A *baby's feet*, like seashells pink,

Might tempt, should *heaven* see meet,

An angel's lips to *kiss*, we think,

A *baby's feet*.

Algernon Charles Swinburne

Where did you come from, baby dear?

Out of the everywhere into here.

Where did you get those eyes so blue?

Out of the sky as I came through.

What makes the light in them sparkle and spin?

Some of the starry spikes left in.

Where did you get that little tear?

I found it waiting when I got here.

What makes your forehead so smooth and high?

A soft hand stroked it as I went by.

George MacDonald

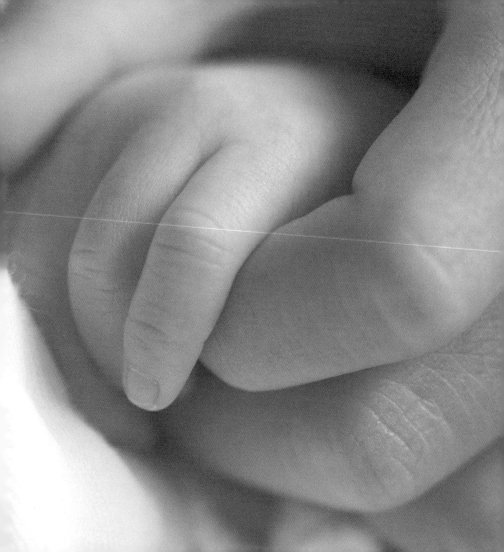

People who *say*
they sleep like a *baby*
usually don't have one.

Leo J. Burke

[God] will never let me stumble, slip or fall.
For he is always watching, never sleeping.

Psalm 121:3–4 TLB

God's ways are as hard to discern

as the pathways of the wind,

and as mysterious as a tiny baby

being formed in a mother's womb.

Ecclesiastes 11:5 NLT

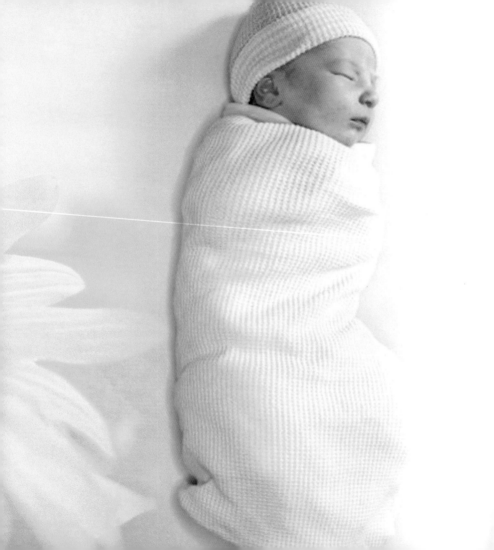

Babies are such a **nice way** t

Before I was born the LORD called me;
from my birth he has made
mention of my name.

Isaiah 49:1 NIV

little LOVE

tart people.   Don Herrold

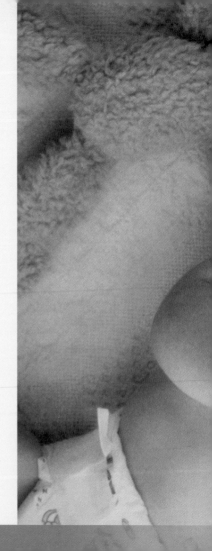

LORD, our LORD,

how majestic is your name in the

whole earth!

You have made your glory higher

than the heavens.

You have made sure that children

and infants praise you.

Psalm 8:1–2 NIrV

It *sometimes* happens, even in the best of families, that a baby is born. This is not necessarily cause for alarm. The impotant thing is to keep your wits about you and borrow some money.

Elinor Goulding Smith

Families **with babies** and

families **without babies**

are **sorry** for each other.

Edgar Howe

Don't you see
that children are
GOD's best gift?
the fruit of the womb
his generous legacy?

Psalm 127:3 THE MESSAGE

Where did you come from, baby dear?

Out of the everywhere into here.

What makes your cheek like a warm white rose?

I saw something better than any one knows.

Whence that three-cornered smile of bliss?

Three angels gave me at once a kiss.

Where did you get this pearly ear?

God spoke, and it came out to hear.

Where did you get those arms and hands?

Love made itself into bonds and bands.

George MacDonald

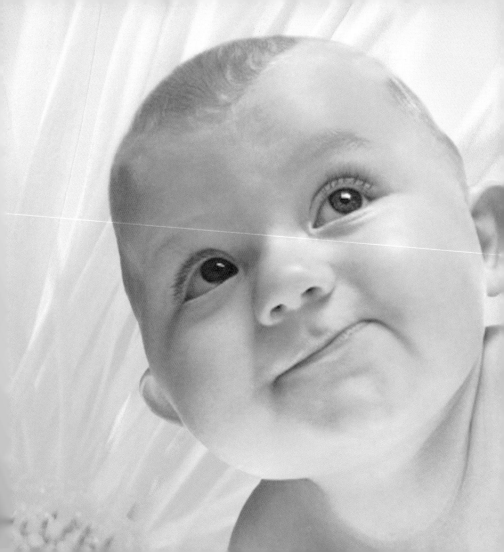

Babies are always more **trouble**

than you thought—and

more **wonderful**.

Charles Osgood

Whatever is good and perfect comes to
us from God, the Creator of all light.

James 1:17 TLB

A *woman* giving birth

to a baby has pain.

This is because her time

to give birth has come.

But when her baby is born,

she forgets the pain.

She forgets because she is

so happy that a baby

has been born into the world.

John 16:21 NIrV

Jesus said, "Let the little children come to Me, and do not forbid them; for of such is the kingdom of heaven."

Matthew 19:14 NKJV

A **baby** is a blank cheque made payable to the human race.

Barbara Christine Seifert

The *Savior*—yes, the
Messiah, the Lord—has been born
tonight in Bethlehem!
How will you recognize him?
You will find a baby
wrapped in a blanket,
lying in a manger!

Luke 2:11–12 TLB

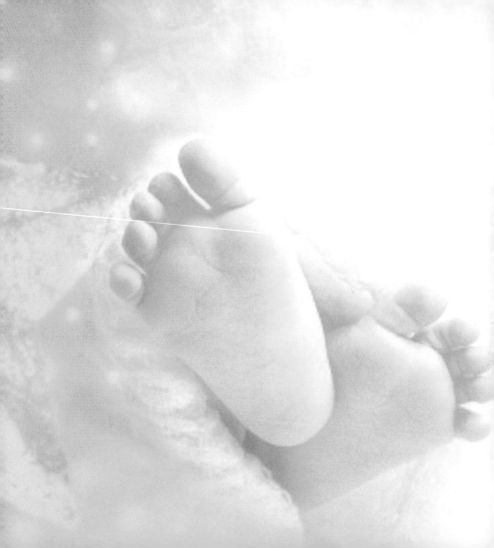

If your **baby** is "beautiful and perfect, never cries or fusses, sleeps on schedule and **burps** on demand, an **angel** all the time," you're the **grandma**.

Teresa Bloomingdale

little ANGEL

A **baby** is God's opinion
that the **world** should go on.

Carl Sandburg

Grandparents are proud
of their grandchildren.

Proverbs 17:6 GNT

...ORD OF **BIRT**...

...hold the office of.........................

...red by law to be k.........said City...

.....18, 19...

E, SURNAME AND BIRTHPLACE

Where did you come from, baby dear?

Out of the everywhere into here.

Feet, whence did you come, you darling things?

From the same box as the cherubs' wings.

How did they all just come to be you?

God thought about me, and so I grew.

But how did you come to us, you dear?

God thought about you, and so I am here.

George MacDonald

Who is getting more **pleasure**
from the rocking,

baby or **me**?

Nancy Thayer

May the righteous be glad and
rejoice before God;
may they be happy and joyful.

Psalm 68:3 NIV

Oh, let GOD enlarge your
families—giving growth to you,
growth to your children.
May you be blessed by GOD,
by GOD, who made heaven
and earth.

Psalm 115:14–15 THE MESSAGE

Your hands have made me and fashioned me;
Give me understanding, that I may learn
Your commandments.

Psalm 119:73 NKJV

Only a *baby* small....

One chubby nose;

Only two *little* hands,

Ten little toes.

Matthias Barr

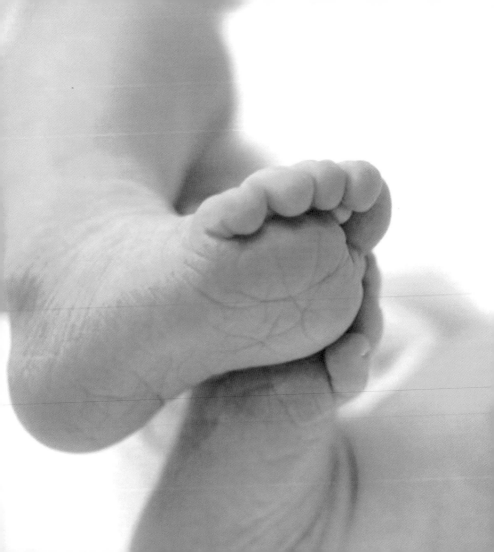

When you look at a baby, it's just that: a body you can look at and touch. But the person who takes shape within is formed by something you can't see and touch—the Spirit— and becomes a living spirit.

John 3:6 THE MESSAGE

In the sheltered

simplicity of the first

days after a baby is

born, one sees again

the magical closed

circle, the miraculous

sense of two people

existing only for

each other.

Anne Morrow Lindbergh

Little Fingers Little Toes
ISBN 1-40378-441-8

Copyright © 2009 Creative Edge, LLC.
Franklin, Tennessee 37027

Published in 2009 by Creative Edge, LLC. Franklin, Tennessee 37027
The CREATIVE EDGE name is a trademark of Dalmatian Publishing Group,
Franklin, Tennessee 37027

Editor: Lila Empson
Compiler: Snapdragon Editorial Group, Inc., Tulsa, Oklahoma
Design: Diane Whisner, Tulsa, Oklahoma

Printed in China.

CE12137/0709

Not flesh of my flesh,

Nor bone of my bone,

But still miraculously my own.

Never forget for a single minute,

You didn't grow under my heart,

But in it!

Fleur Conkling Heyliger

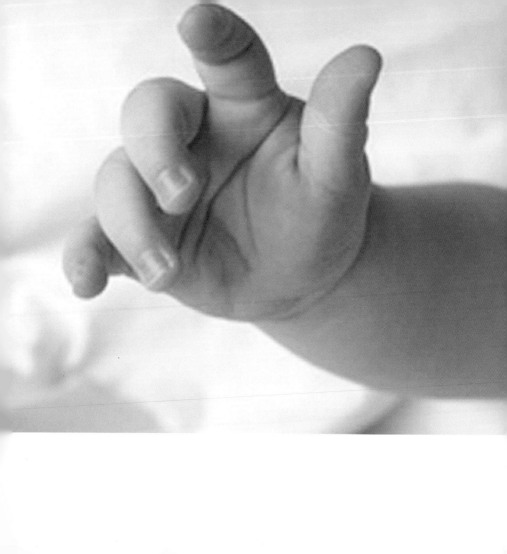

Who may ascend into the hill of the LORD?
Or who may stand in His holy place?
He who has clean hands and a pure heart.

Psalm 24:3–4 NKJV

The *sweetest* flowers in all the world—a baby's hands.

Algernon Charles Swinburne